You Are Beyond Who You Are

Good Thoughts

Good Words   *Good Deeds*

by
Bahram Spitama

 FriesenPress

One Printers Way
Altona, MB R0G 0B0
Canada

www.friesenpress.com

ISBN
978-1-03-919873-9 (Hardcover)
978-1-03-919872-2 (Paperback)
978-1-03-919874-6 (eBook)

1. RELIGION, ZOROASTRIANISM

Distributed to the trade by The Ingram Book Company

Table of Contents

About the Author

BAHRAM MOTERASSED (Spitama)[1] has been a psycho-therapist for thirty years, incorporating Eastern spirituality into his practice. He has a BA in psychology and a master's degree in marriage and family therapy. He has studied and practised Sufism, Buddhism, Yoga, Mazdaism, Christianity, Kabbalah, and has participated in sweat lodges in the tradition of the Indigenous peoples of Canada. He has also practised and taught meditation courses for more than thirty years.

---

1   Spitama is chosen here because of the author's immense love and respect for the wisdom of Zarathustra Spitama.

Acknowledgements

I would like to dedicate this book to my family in Canada and in Iran for their influence in my life. I am thankful for my Persian culture, which has taught me the wisdom of the East. I am indebted to the West and to Western culture and its people, who have hosted me kindly and lovingly over the past forty years of my life. I feel fortunate to have gained the wisdom of both the East and the West, like an eagle that has two wings, allowing me to fly as high as I have courage to. Together, these two cultures are like the right side and the left side of my brain. They help me to see and to understand life from a different point of view. They are not contradicting each other; rather, they are complementary to one another. I am so grateful to be exposed to both.

This book is dedicated to my mentor, John Millar. He was an authentic and very real person. Serving as my clinical supervisor, he became a father figure and a friend over many years. Like a Zen master, he was direct and right to the point, a truly wise man. Peace be with his soul. It is also dedicated to the French linguistic scholar Abraham Anquetil-Duperron (1731–1805)—who translated the *Gathas* (Zarathustra's sublime songs) so that we now have a clear understanding of the wisdom of Zarathustra for the first time after thousands of years.

Introduction

Who Am I?

"The life that is unexamined is not worth living."

Socrates

In our quest for material possessions, like computers, cars, or houses, it's common to seek information about their overall quality before making a purchase. We're interested in detail such as their type, model, and price. Interestingly, in our daily lives, we frequently use the word "I" more than any other, yet often without deeply considering who this "I" truly is. It's odd that we spend so much energy learning about things outside ourselves, yet we don't know ourselves well. It's strange that we live in our bodies for many years, but we rarely think about who's inside. How many of us would slow down from our busy lives to learn about ourselves? How often do we stop and ask why we're here and what happens after we're gone?

Do we take the time to examine whether there is more to us than our physical body? Are we just the body? We realize that our bodies change continuously throughout the years. The body that we had as a child was very different from our teenage years or in our old age. Science has proven that all our cells are replaced totally every seven years. In fact, the body we have now is no longer the same as the one we had at birth. Despite all the physical changes, there is still a part of us that remains untouched and original. What is this that remains untouched?

We rarely think about the mystery behind our physical functioning. Most of us agree that we don't choose to circulate our blood or digest the food we eat. Have we questioned who is really beating our hearts, inhaling and exhaling the breath, or healing our wounds? Who is the one who puts us to sleep and wakes us up every morning? Who is the one asking these questions? Is it only the mind asking, or is there something in each of us that yearns to be sought? Who is really the questioner behind all these questions?

How often do we take the time to inquire and search for our true self beyond our profession, gender, nationality, or name? We attempt to answer the question of who we are by hanging onto certain labels, roles, and ownerships. We describe who we are in a limited form, such as Jim, father, male, Canadian, dentist, middle-aged, or Christian. But did not we exist before we were given a name? Don't we still exist even though we change our jobs, hobbies, roles, and relationships?

Although many definitions of who we are provide an illusion of permanency of our identities, are they really us? We can lose our jobs or retire, but we will still exist. We existed before having our children and becoming a parent, so who we are is not really a parent. Who we are is constantly changing. We can be kind or active at one point and be angry and passive at another point. A very kind and gentle person can also surprise others by behaving totally unpredictably at some point.

Human beings are the most complex creatures in the animal kingdom. We are the only creatures who can think and reflect on the mystery of existence. In fact, what makes us human is our ability to inquire about the true meaning of our being. However, most of us become so preoccupied with all kinds of activities and worldly affairs that constrain us from reflecting on our true nature, until we come to a stage in our life when our pleasure, ambition, and striving start to wear on us and invite us to yearn for a deeper meaning to our existence.

There is a deep longing within us that is often experienced as boredom. This boredom manifests as a sense of unease, a feeling of lack, or of something missing. There is a fundamental reality that we may ignore: We are born alone, and we die alone. We are the centre of all the changes happening around us, either daily or throughout our life span. We may try to avoid this uncomfortable feeling by distracting ourselves with television or by trying to fill the emptiness with sex, drugs, or alcohol. Yet nothing we do seems to fill this aching void within.

This hunger cannot be satisfied with friendly chatter or external pursuits, but rather by learning to "sit alone in a quiet room." The root of this internal void is that we have a relationship with many people or things, but we don't have one with ourselves. There is a stranger within us who is called "me." We often fill our days with activities. Some of our activities are the result of obligations of family and work, while other activities are simply created to distract us from ourselves. We lose ourselves in the circumstances of our daily lives. There is a saying that goes, "you can run, but you cannot hide." We can hide ourselves from others, but we cannot hide ourselves from ourselves. "Everywhere we go, there we are."

Sooner or later, our pleasures, pains, and striving may start to wear on us and lose their meaning. We want a deeper understanding of our existence. This potent question often ignites a burning desire to remember a forgotten secret and discover the source of this deep longing. A thirst arises that can no longer be ignored and can no longer be quenched by worldly pleasures or entertainment. The thirst is to "know thyself" and to remember oneself on a deeper level. Once, I went to see a client in the hospital who had only a few days to live. She said, "All the investment that I made outside of myself to bring social, relational, and political changes to my outer circumstances are pointless at this time. I am facing a part of myself that I never inquired to know throughout my life span. There is a stranger within me that I am forced to face, and I cannot escape any longer."

Western psychology has limited itself to understanding oneself through the study of human personality, which is a by-product of our culture and our environment. Modern psychology can only take us deep into the human psyche, but it has failed to take us deep into the essence of our being, as Eastern mystics do. Although Western psychology and psychiatry have advanced our knowledge and understanding of human cognition—the mind, behaviours, emotions, and the nervous system—they have neglected to take us beyond our conventional, biological, and societal identities. Most of modern psychology is limited to examining only the superficial part of ourselves. It has failed to take us beyond societal norms. Most of our understanding of human beings is based on dysfunctional and "abnormal" human characteristics rather than the investigation on what it is to be a healthy human being.

Western psychology has aimed to lead people back to a sense of normalcy. However, we human beings are not born to be just normal and vegetate in our lives. Everything in the universe is complete. It works harmoniously at an unconscious level and incorporates certain patterns, such as a horse being born and dying as a horse or a rose following the same life cycle. Unlike other creatures, we are born incomplete. Our purpose is to become whole. We are here to uncover the universe's imprint within us, to tap into our boundless potential, and to transcend our temporal existence for eternity. Our journey involves moving from unconsciousness to full consciousness, awakening our true selves.

When we say "I," where do we look to find the self? Where is "I"? Is it the body, heart, emotion, mind, career, physical appearance, ethnicity, or gender? Aside from our names, ethnicity, religion, roles, and culture, there is a part of us that is beyond the earthly level. A part that is always there in the background, witnessing and observing our existence. A part that needs to be remembered and grow to be "Godlike." Recognizing and knowing the "Godly" part of ourselves can lead us to discover something higher within us rather than outside of us. This realization and recognition are called "awakening."

In this book, I am inviting you to travel the journey of self-discovery based on the ancient teachings and wisdom of Zarathustra. Throughout history, Zarathustra's teachings have shaped and impacted different cultures and belief systems in a wide variety of ways worldwide. Zarathustra lived about five thousand years ago in Persia (Iran).[2] He challenged us to look at ourselves not as who we are, but as who we can become. His aim for humanity was for us to transcend to become higher, conscious beings. And those higher human beings are hidden within us.

We are like a ladder. We need to climb up the steps of our beings in order to reach the treasure of our full consciousness. Then, we are not human anymore. We become closer to God, Ahura Mazda—the Ultimate Consciousness, the Supreme Wisdom. His philosophy eventually established Zoroastrianism as the dominant religion in Persia. It remained the state religion of the empire until about the seventh century (CE), when Muslims conquered Persia.

Zarathustra's dream was to see Earth flourishing with conscious human beings. He encouraged us to transform into different, not just improved, individuals. His concern wasn't improving humanity or changing society's structure. The quest for a better personality, more advanced technology, or luxurious possessions doesn't give us wisdom, kindness, or love. These things don't automatically make us conscious beings, no matter how wealthy or surrounded by material possessions we are. Zarathustra points us toward a humanity rooted in awareness and wisdom.

Zarathustra was like a gardener. He spread the seeds of his wisdom into the soil of our existence. He saw in us the potential to go beyond ourselves. We are not meant to creep and crawl on

2   The name officially changed from Persia to Iran in 1935.

Earth like a caterpillar. We are meant to transcend ourselves and fly to the ultimate heights like a butterfly. His teaching is a religion of becoming, not just existing and vegetating. Religion in his view doesn't mean robotic rituals or obeying certain commands. Religion in his perspective doesn't mean going to the temple or searching for something outside of ourselves.

Zarathustra did not intend to create an organized religion. His teaching is organic. It is simply to live authentically and spontaneously in every moment of our lives. He does not give us a script to follow word for word. His approach is like a goose flying south without leaving any footprint. Religion for him means to live from our essence, to be true to our true self, keeping in mind good thoughts, good words, and good deeds in our daily activities and in our life span.

Glossary

Ahriman	Wicked thought/spirit/energy/anger Angra Mainyu in the *Gathas,* Satan in English
Ahura Mazda	The Sublime Wisdom, the Essence The Supreme Consciousness, God in English both masculine and feminine *Ahura*: masculine, consciousness, light *Mazda*: feminine, wisdom, life
Amesha Spenta	Immortal Bounteous; seven attributes of Ahura Mazda
Angra Mainyu	The spirit of ignorance, unconsciousness Wickedness, anger in English, Ahriman, Satan in English
Armaiti	Devotion, love, peace
Asha/Artha	Harmony, balance, *art* in English, harmony
Daena	Conscience, inner wisdom and morality, inner eyes *Deen/Din*: Religion in Persian
Fravashi	Authentic self, true self/spirit, our essence, "I," angel, guardian angel in English, holy souls

Gathas	Songs, the sublime songs of Zarathustra Composed by himself about five thousand years ago, the only surviving Indo-European language
Khordad	Perfection, wholeness, integrity, completion
Magi	The followers of Zarathustra's wisdom teaching, seeker of wisdom, *Moghan* in Persian
Mainyu	*Mind* in English, spirit, energy, way of thinking
Murdad	Eternal, deathless, immortal
Serosha	Conscience, voice, inner voice
Shahrewar	Willpower, inner discipline and control
Spenta	Sacred, holy, progressive
Spenta Mainyu	Sacred wisdom, good mind, progressive mentality, Holy Spirit in English
Spitama	Zarathustra, also known as meaning "pure"
Zarathustra	Zarathustra was an enlightened person who lived about five thousand years ago in Persia (Iran), the founder of the Zoroastrian religion and Mazdaism (Seeker of Wisdom)

CHAPTER 1
Know Thyself

"Knowing others is wisdom;
knowing yourself is enlightenment."

Lao Tzu

Ancient wisdom counsels us to "know thyself." However, many of us rarely slow down long enough to truly examine our true selves. We are too busy building careers, studying facts, or getting lost in the constellation of faraway stars. In most cases, human beings are much more interested in becoming acquainted with other people than getting to know the stranger that lies within themselves. We tend to think of ourselves as one unified and integrated self. However, when we look deeply into ourselves, we find multiple "I's." Our sense of "I" is often fragmented depending on our context. Who we are varies depending on the moment and is affected by our relationships, our roles, our emotions, our thoughts, and our own self-image.

Death becomes like a mirror that forces us to look at ourselves. We feel trapped in death because we cannot distract or ignore our true self anymore. If we have not self-inquired throughout our lives, we look into the mirror of death at the stranger in front of us and ask ourselves, "Who am I?" We may realize that we wasted our life by pursuing unnecessary goals and achievements while ignoring knowing ourselves as the priority. We may realize at the point of death that all the collected identities were nothing. They were just some toys for children to play with. They were not real.

We don't know what we want and our true propose in life. How can we know what we want when we don't know who we are? It is like buying a pair of shoes online without knowing the size of our feet. We first need to know our size before ordering the shoes.

From our childhood, we are told who we are as we grow, for example: He is a boy, Jimmy, Christian, tall, smart, or polite. On his first day of school, the teacher asks the students to introduce themselves. When she reaches Jimmy, she asks his name. He says, "Jimmy." She asks, "Jimmy who?" He says, "Jimmy Don't." Aren't we all Jimmy Don't, collecting many "do's" and "don'ts" in our lives like a burdened camel?

As a child, we begin to view a physical separation between ourselves and our surroundings and caregivers. This sense of separation develops a false sense of identity—me vs. others. Gradually, we start collecting false ideas and concepts of who we are based on a sense of separation and how others perceive us. As our identities begin to shape, we associate ourselves more with our personalities. As a result, we move further and further away from our true self—our "essence."

Every person has two fundamental parts inside of them. One is how we think and view ourselves (personality or ego). The other is who we truly are (essence). We live our lives without being aware of our essence and the authentic part of ourselves. It is like we are divided into two parts: I and am—I-am. The "I" is our ego, our self-image, our identity, our personality. The "am" is the essence and authentic part of ourselves that connects us to our being, origin, existence, and life. We often associate ourselves with the "I" and the person we understand ourselves to be or how others view us. If we remain identified with who we think we are in our personality, we will never come to know our true inner being.

To inquire further into the statement of "knowing thyself," let's first differentiate our personality (ego) from the authentic self (essence). Although our personalities are formed based on certain genetic factors and cultural and social circumstances, there is another self within us that has no earthly formation or description. We can only see that part of ourselves through the inner eyes and internal experiences. It is the path of self-observation and awareness.

Personality vs. Essence

"You ask me how I became a madman. It happened thus: One day, long before many gods were born, I woke from a deep sleep and found all my masks were stolen—the seven masks I have fashioned and worn in seven lives—I ran maskless through the crowded streets shouting, 'Thieves, thieves, the cursed thieves.'

Men and women laughed at me and some ran to their houses in fear of me.

And when I reached the marketplace, a youth standing on a housetop cried, 'He is a madman.' I looked up to behold him; the sun kissed my own naked face for the first time. For the first time the sun kissed my own naked face and my soul was inflamed with love for the sun, and I wanted my masks no more. And as if in a trance I cried, 'Blessed, blessed are the thieves who stole my masks.'

Thus I became a madman.

And I have found both freedom and safety in my madness; the freedom of loneliness and the safety from being understood, for those who understand us enslave something in us.

But let me not be too proud of my safety. Even a thief in a jail is safe from another thief." [3]

While there are many theories about human personalities from different schools of psychology, we first need to know what the term personality means. Personality comes from Greek dramas—*persona*. It refers to a theatrical mask worn by performers according to their roles in ancient Greece. In those dramas, each player would have to wear a mask. They used to call the mask a persona, and the character created by that mask was called the personality. They were acting out something they were not. Similar to the mask, our personality means that which we are not. Our true face and self are hidden behind it.

3   Gibran, Kahlil. The Madman: His Parables and Poems. New York: A.A. Knopf, 1918.

Our persona (personality) is the mask that we wear in order to present ourselves according to our social settings. Just as the Greek actors whose real faces were covered by the mask (persona), our real self is masked by our personality. It is like a cloud blocking the sun. Personality is limited, and it creates an illusion of separation between us and our surroundings. It also gives a false idea of who we really are. Personality is like a fake coin. It looks real, but it does not have any value. Our personality is a counterfeit version of ourselves.

As our identities began to shape, we moved further and further away from our true self. It is like the ancient Greek actors who may start forgetting their original faces under the masks (persona). They may begin to identify more with the masks and their roles on the stage than with who they truly are. One may play the role of a king on the stage, and he may still act like a king when he leaves the theatre in real life. Indeed, we all become like actors trying to fit into a role on the stage of life and finding an appropriate script to perform our lives accordingly.

Although our environment and culture are important contributions to the formation of our personalities, we cannot deny the genetic blueprint of our personality at birth. Our environment forms us differently from each other in life. People who have children know well that each of their children are born with some predisposition and personality. Each child is born with a certain genetic temperament that influences the child's approach and interaction to the world. Most psychologists agree that both temperament (nature) and environment (nurture) are important factors that influence the development of one's personality.

The Pearl inside the Oyster Shell

In order to come to know our essence and true self, we need to drop all the clothes of the personality. In Zen, it is called finding our original face. Yeshua (Jesus in Greek)[4] was said to become a child again. The clothes of personality need to be dropped not only externally, but also internally—in our minds—in how we perceive ourselves. When we are in touch with our essence, there is a sense of unity and wholeness. In essence, we are all one. In personality, we are many and fractured. If we pour water into different shaped containers, add colours to them, and freeze them, the ice cubes are all different shapes and colours, but they all have the same source—water.

When we realize that the masks—our personality— are just a social identity, we can drop them any time and become naked to our being and our essence. There must be an inner separation within us between our essence and personality. The inner separation helps us see our personality through the eyes of the essence—the inner eyes. By emptying ourselves of the personality, the essence begins to emerge. It is like we have a rose garden, but there are too many weeds that prevent us from seeing the roses. First, we need to distinguish the roses

---

4   The name Yeshua rather than Jesus has been chosen for this book. It needs to be pointed out that Jesus's real name was "Yeshua" in Hebrew and Joshua in English. The name Jesus was given to him by the Greeks years after his crucifixion. However, Jesus's real name was "Yeshua." https://en.wikipedia.org/wiki/Jesus_(name)

from the weeds. Then, by removing and emptying the garden of the weeds, the roses become evident. Personality is like the weeds surrounding the essence in the garden of our being. Personality is like a dark cloud that blocks the sun. The sun is always there to give us true life, light, and warmth. However, the clouds are obstacles to the sun.

Disassociating oneself from personality brings authenticity since personality is false, pseudo, fake, and phony. We were not born with it. It was imposed on us after birth from the outside. However, our essence is what we bring into the world from beyond. Essence is not egoistic. In contrast to personality, it does not have a sense of "I"; it is pure "am-ness." It carries the wisdom of existence and contains the seed of our higher being. Knowing our essence means knowing the immortal part of ourselves. The body, mind, emotions, and all our identities die one day, but there is a part within that does not have any beginning nor ending. It is the *alpha* and the *omega*.

One does not need external proof or scientific fact to realize that. It is an inner realization and experience. It is connecting with a part of ourselves that is conscious, an observer, and a witness to what is happening outside and inside us. As we connect more and more to our essence, a different level of consciousness and awareness begins to emerge that is separate from our personality and identity.

As long as we are attached to our personality, we repress the essence, and we are not real. The authentic part in us remains in darkness, like the sun covered by a cloud. We are stuck as who we are. We become frozen to our idea of who we are. We refuse to see ourselves as who we really are. Our patterns and behaviours are well predicted and never change. We think that we are unpredictable human beings. We are not. Who we are today is as a result of yesterday. Tomorrow's behaviour is based on who we were yesterday and today. There is a saying that goes, "The definition of insanity is doing the same thing over and over and expecting different results."

At times, we may change a bit by getting rid of one mask and wearing a different mask, pretending to be a different actor. There is a sense of safety and security in wearing the mask. We gain recognition, acceptance, respect, and predictability. In essence, no one can say who we are, except ourselves. It is like nobody can know you are thirsty or hungry except you. No one else lives inside you except you. Have you noticed that it does not matter with whom you are or where you are, you never experience anything outside of yourself? You are always inside, no matter when, where, or with whom you are. We are always inside a box called our body. So, how can someone know you more than you know yourself when you are conscious and aware within?

The Four Sources of Self-Identity

When we go within, we find four sources of identification. Inside, it is like we have a four-storey house that we live in: our body, emotions, mind, and essence (true self).

1. Body: We often think we are what we look like. Since we live in our bodies, we have the illusion that we are our bodies. We take pride and identify ourselves by our body image, beauty, shape, or health. We get a sense of self-identity from our clothes, hairstyle, makeup, or body shape. If we reflect deeply, we don't know much about the body. We only get a perspective of our bodies by looking at it in a mirror or a picture. The perspective we have of our bodies is very external. We hardly look at the body from within.

As mentioned earlier, all the cells in the body now are totally different from the ones seven years ago. We age, and our bodies transform throughout our lives. Due to illness or accident, we may lose some of our body's organs, or they become dysfunctional. We don't say that we are our houses because we live in them. We know who we are despite the different houses we live in. Have we ever questioned who really lives inside our bodies? One day we are born, and we are destined to eventually die. Do we have only a momentary existence, like a shooting star, and are we then totally erased from the universe when the body dies? Or is there a part in us beyond any form, shape, or matter?

The body dies, but life never dies. Life is like energy. It cannot be created or destroyed. It only shifts from one form of energy to another. It is like a wave in the ocean. Waves come and go, but the ocean remains the same. The ocean does not die because a wave has disappeared. Life existed before the body and will continue after.

2. Emotion: Some of us may identify ourselves with our emotions. For example, if we are prone to anger, we may think of ourselves as an angry person. If we are often sad, we may think of ourselves as a depressed or lonely person. If we are generally kind, we may believe we are a kind person. But what happens to our identities when we say an unkind thing? Are we still a kind person? Or do we now identify ourselves as an unkind or "bad" person?

One of the major issues in mental health is the label of the diagnosis. The diagnosis might be: "You are depressed." "You are anxious." "You are anorexic." Is it true? The diagnosis is like a tattoo engraved on the person. When someone has the flu, do we say to the person that you are the flu, or do we say you have the flu? When someone has a lung infection, do we say that you are the infection? Or do we say that you have an infection? Similarly, we need to know that we caught depression, anger, anorexia, or borderline. We are not them, and they are not who we are.

Because our thoughts, ideas, and emotions change and shift along with situations and moods, our sense of self can be unstable. We may search for some sense of security and permanency within our emotional instability. We may become entangled with our emotions because they produce a feeling of stability, and many of us cling to the comfort of our familiar lives even if they cause us pain. Our emotional entanglement becomes a self-fulfilling prophecy. Our sadness, anger, misery, or joyfulness becomes our identity. It is interesting in psychotherapy, how even though a person may come to work on their unhappiness, they may resist change because their current state has become their identity. They do not know who they are if they let go of their unhappiness.

3. Mind: Descartes said, "I think, therefore I am." We identify with our thoughts so much that we refuse to view ourselves apart from our mind. The mind is the mental function of the brain. Our brains gather information from the five senses (sight, hearing, taste, smell, and touch). The mind's role is to obtain knowledge and to understand and process the information through our thoughts, memories, experiences, and five senses. The brain has a form, but the mind is formless. It is like when we see a beautiful flower. The flower is visible, but beauty is an attribute. Beauty is formless, and it cannot be separated from the flower. The brain is visible, but the mind is not and cannot function apart from the brain.

Separation and division are the essence of the mind. The function of mind is to divide any phenomena into a category, a label, or a framework. The mind helps us categorize the world around us in order to understand and communicate more easily with one another. Language is the mind's greatest creation. By labelling and naming everything around us, the mind makes it possible for us to understand each other and express ourselves meaningfully. It also assists us in examining phenomena in a more detailed and precise manner.

For example, when one talks about John Lennon, the mind helps us to recognize him among other people and to distinguish him from Elvis Presley. One knows through the mind's function that a rose is a flower and not a bird or a rock. It helps us think logically and have memories. Thanks to the mind, we can recognize our car in the parking lot, know how to drive it, and find our way back home again.

Although the mind has an important function in serving us, similar to the other parts of our body, it has its limitations. The purpose of the eyes is to see, but they simply cannot hear. The function of the legs is to walk, but they are not able to see. The mind knows the world around us through a lens of concepts, frameworks, and categories. A map is needed to find our destination, but a map is not the territory.

Since the function of the mind is to know things through labels and names, it separates our direct experience from what is. The moment the mind begins to analyze a person, it creates a judgment by placing someone in a certain group or framework. It prevents a person from experiencing anyone fully as they are. Or, when the mind perceives things through language—such as the moment one sees a rose—the mind thinks about the word "rose." As a result, the mind creates a distraction and prevents a person from experiencing the flower fully as it truly is.

Since the mind does not have any direct experience of who we truly are, it creates an idea and concept of the self. Therefore, the mind develops a separate sense of the self than what is. The mind can function with what it knows. As a result, it establishes a sense of identity of who we are with what it knows, such as our gender, social class, age, name, profession, or nationality. Ego (persona) is the mind's false sense of the true self with whatever one identifies. Ego is like a scarecrow. It has the shape and clothes of a person, but it is not real. Our ego is a false sense of reality about ourselves that the mind creates. There is a misconception that ego means selfish. No; ego means any perception one has about themselves. Ego is our false sense of who we think we are.

It is like when we see the moonlight at night. The moon appears to have its own light. Even though we don't see the sun at night, the moonlight does not exist apart from the sun's light. Our brain is like the moon and the mind is like the moonlight. The mind cannot exist without the light of our being (essence). We think that because we are alive, we think. That is not true. People who practise meditation still exist even though they let go of the mind. The mind can be like a magician who can create a false reality out of a deception.

The nature of the mind is division and interpretation. There is no such thing as a silent mind. The mind and silence cannot exist at the same time. It is like darkness and light cannot be together at the same time. One can only be fully present when the mind ceases to be. The less light there is in a room, the darker it becomes. Similarly, the mind prevents the presence of our essence to be experienced.

We can only experience our true self when the mind disappears. Living with this deception gives us a little relief. The connection to our false identity comforts us, like a child holding a teddy bear. Identification with our personality is only needed in the absence of self-knowing. The moment we drop the ego, we face such a vastness that it cannot be defined by any concepts. The ego is like a pacifier that soothes us in the absence of the mother's breast.

4. Essence: The mind attempts to create a permanent personality—a false self—but the true self is not a self at all. The true self is not a self because it does not have any labels or definitions. It is our true existence. We begin to search for our essence when we let go of our ego and become no one. As far as we are identifying ourselves with somebody, we cannot experience the essence. In that nothingness and vacuum of the personality the essence evolves.

There was once a rich merchant who had three sons. He wanted to know which one of his sons was able to run the business after him. He gave them a week to come up with the most wealth that they could and bring it back to him. The oldest was in the farming business and sold many crops and some of the fields to collect his wealth. The middle son was a shepherd and sold some of his animals to show his wealth to his father. The youngest one did not have any career or wealth. By the end of the week, they all presented their wealth to the father. They were all surprised to see that the youngest one brought more money than the other ones.

Everyone asked the youngest one how he came up with so much money. He said that a rich man gave most of his wealth to him, and he did not know why. The other brothers went to the rich man and asked him why he gave most of his wealth to their youngest brother. He said that he had gone to a doctor and was told that he had a terminal illness. He had only a few months to live. The doctor told him that "nothing" can help him at this time.

He said that when he left the doctor's office, he promised that if he found a cure for his illness, he would give away most of his wealth. He said that he was walking in the market and saw their younger brother had a table at the market. He had a bag on the table to sell. It said on the bag: "Nothing for sale." The rich man said he was very happy to find the cure for his illness since the doctor had told him "nothing" could help him. We need to get to a point where there is nothing left in us to claim as "I." Only in that "nothingness" can we find our cure to connect with the true self.

Our essence is like a mirror that reflects many faces in front of it without being entangled with any of them. If a happy person stands in front of the mirror, it does not make the mirror happy. The mirror only reflects what is in front of it. It will let go of the image as soon as the person walks away from it. Similarly, the essence can never be hurt, sad, or happy. It reflects whatever is in front of it without being identified with any physical appearances, emotions, or thoughts.

Personality can be described, but essence is unexplainable and indescribable. It is our nature that we are born with, similar to the elements of hydrogen and oxygen in water. It is like how one can explain the colour green. There is no way to measure green based on smell, height, weight, or sound. Can you explain green to a blind person? No; one is required to see it and to experience it.

Above every ordinary self, there is a higher self waiting to be born. However, one needs to reach a higher level of existence and open the door to experience the true self and the Supreme Being—Ahura Mazda. Zarathustra opened the door and experienced himself beyond his ordinary self. At that space of his being, he experienced the Supreme Essence, the essence of all essence. And he invited and guided all of us to reach that level of his experience.[5]

He found his real being like a sun shining in his existence. The self was not part of his body, nor it was a necessary condition with which to identify himself. His existence and

5   Gathas: Yasna 31.8, Gathas: Yasna 45.8

consciousness were like a river merged with the ocean—the Supreme Consciousness, Ahura Mazda.

The *Fravashi* Symbol—The Authentic Self

*Figure #1. Fravashi—*Our Essence

Within us, there exists a part of Ahura Mazda known as *fravashi*—our true essence. It is a spirit that existed before our current life and will endure after death. *Fravashi* is considered sacred. It predates the universe's creation and can be envisioned as a human-like figure with two wings. In Mazdaism, fravashi carries significant symbolism, representing our true self, our real self, and even a connection to the divine self.

Most often, we are not aware of—or connected with—our true self (*fravashi*). We are born with our essence, but it is like a hidden seed until we nurture and develop it. The path to spiritual life doesn't rely on personality since it mainly operates in society. An apple seed won't grow into an apple tree unless we plant it in the soil, provide water, and care for it. Growing the seed into a tree requires effort and attention. Eventually, when the tree matures, it bears fruit—apples. But this growth process can't happen unless we nurture the seed. Similarly, we must cultivate the seed of fravashi in our consciousness. We need to consistently nurture and tend to it through our thoughts, words, and actions to fully develop it into a "Mazda-like" state.

Our true self is like a dimmer switch. It starts from a dark and low point, and as we gradually increase its brightness, our inner world becomes fully illuminated. Through embracing our authentic self, our awareness expands, making us more receptive to Mazda's love and wisdom. Hence, in our spiritual journey, the most crucial task is to be open and receptive to Mazda's presence within us. Surrendering is essential for spiritual growth. Zarathustra emphasizes surrendering not to any specific person or belief, but rather to divine love and consciousness.

The symbol of *fravashi* shows a person with wings like an eagle, representing the journey toward our ultimate essence. Here is what each aspect of the symbol signifies:

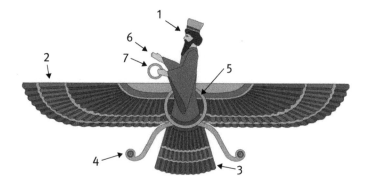

Figure #2. The meaning of *fravashi*

1. **Wisdom of Age:** The face represents an elderly individual who has gained wisdom, looking forward to growth and freedom while leaving ignorance behind.

2. **Three Principles of Zarathustra:** The upper wings consist of three layers representing Zarathustra's three principles: good thoughts, good words, and good deeds.

3. **Three Opposing Forces:** The lower part of the symbol represents three separate elements: wicked thoughts, wicked words, and wicked deeds. These are associated with negative paths leading to misfortune and unhappiness.

4. **Positive and Negative Forces:** The loops on either side of *fravashi* represent positive forces (Sacred Wisdom—Spenta Mainyu) and negative forces (Wicked Force—Ahriman, Satan, Angra Mainyu). The positive loop faces forward, signifying progress toward goodness, while the negative loop at the back signifies turning away from wickedness.

5. **Immortal Spirit, Eternal Universe:** The central circle around *fravashi*'s trunk symbolizes the immortal nature of the spirit, reflecting eternity without a beginning or end.

6. **Choosing the Right Path:** One of the elderly figure's hands points upward, representing the human effort needed to grow and fulfill their potential.

7. **Path of Loyalty and Faithfulness:** A ring is present, symbolizing a covenant for faithfulness and loyalty to the path of goodness and wisdom, much like a wedding promise.

CHAPTER 2
Motivating Forces

The four layers of our self-identities were explored briefly in the previous chapter. However, the question can be asked: What motivates us in our lives based on the different senses of self that we have? How do we make choices in our lives? And what is the motivation behind our choices?

Zarathustra speaks of a twin force at work in the world and in human consciousness. The first one is *Spenta Mainyu*, the Good Mind (Sacred Wisdom), which wants to pull us to a higher consciousness (Wisdom). This is the force of progression. The other force is called *Angra Mainyu*, the Wicked Mind, (*Ahriman*). This internal force wants to pull us down to ignorance, destruction, and unconsciousness. This is the spirit of stagnation and deception.[6] Although Zarathustra teaches us about two forces in the human mind (Conscious Mind and Wicked Mind), these two forces are connected and not in cosmic battle with one another or in a dualistic framework.

We humans grow and learn through our experiences of these two forces, forces that offer us choices. We don't know what is

6   Gathas: Yasna 30.3

good unless we experience something bad. We don't know love unless we know hate. They're related in a complementary position, not in opposition. It is similar to two sides of a coin. You cannot take one side of a coin and destroy it and forget about the other side of the coin. Both exist simultaneously. That is what Zarathustra was saying when he said that everything has its own polarity called twin spirits.

Everything in existence is created in pairs, and life on earth is based on the connection between those twin spirits and the choices that we make. Some of the choices that we make will give us satisfaction and fulfillment, and others will cause us pain and suffering. Do I need to go to work or stay at home? Do I need to exercise or just sit on the couch and watch TV? Do I want to marry or be single? Am I going to drive while I am under the influence or take a taxi? Do I need to continue the current argument that I have with my spouse or let it go? Our existence as human beings is designed at birth in a position of continually having to make choices.[7]

However, most of the choices that we make are unconscious and reactive based on two fundamental forces: either the force of attraction or the force of repulsion. We desire something when we are attracted to it. And we pull away from and detest something when we are afraid or dislike it. Our choices are not conscious; rather, they are mechanical and reactive. We increase our investment and connection because of the pleasure and reward that we receive. On the other hand, we reduce our activities and interests to avoid pain and suffering.

----

7   Gathas: Yasna 53.2

Our motivations are based on receiving the maximum rewards and reducing punishment or pain. Our ultimate goal is to be in a state of infinite joy and happiness, either physically, emotionally, psychologically, financially, relationally, or spiritually. We were told to live our lives in pursuit of everlasting happiness in heaven or enlightenment. And we were warned to avoid activities that bring us suffering in hell, bad karma, or eternal punishment. Attraction and repulsion are the sources of love and fear in most of us. At the same time, we react based on the result and outcome of our choices. We get angry when we do not get satisfaction from what we desire. We remove ourselves from what we are afraid of. Anxiety is the cause of excess worry and fear that we have of a phenomenon that may prevent us from being engaged in life. The motivational forces behind our attractions are rooted within our need, desire, devotion, and will.

Needs, Desires, Devotion, and Will

Needs: Abraham Maslow, a well-known psychologist, introduced the idea of a hierarchy of needs as a core source of human motivation. He organized human needs into a pyramid ranging from basic necessities, such as food and water, to higher aspirations, such as self-fulfillment and actualization. According to Maslow, once our basic needs are fulfilled, we turn our attention to fulfilling higher-level needs.

However, Maslow's concept is very limited and not fully accurate. He only saw needs as a source of human motivation and neglected to see desires, love, devotion, and will as other sources of our motivation. When we talk about needs, we should realize that our needs are only applicable in a lower self of human beings. When we think about our lives, our needs are few and are meant for our survival. We need food, water, reproduction, shelter, clothes, and safety. The main purpose of our lower self is associated with our bodily function. It is to satisfy our physiological needs in order to survive.

The duty of the lower self is to nourish the body (food, air, water) and protect it against any danger. The physical self is required to fulfill other bodily needs, such as securing shelter, a mate, and protection. Without fulfilling those needs, we cannot survive and continue our existence on Earth. The physical needs are essential for our livelihood and longevity. Without those needs, we cannot survive. The job of the lower self is to make sure the physiological needs are met. But it is important to realize that the higher self has desires. It functions based on what it wants, not what it needs. Our needs are necessary; our wants are important to us. We cannot survive without meeting our needs. But we can survive if we don't get what we want.

Desires (wants): In terms of our emotional and intellectual selves, we don't have needs. We function based on desires and wants. I need food, but I don't need to be respected. I want and desire respect. I need to breathe, but I don't need a new TV or to be a dentist. I desire and want them. We are required to distinguish their needs from their desires. Needs are few, but desires are limitless. If we pay attention to advertisements, we notice that what is presented to viewers are only desires, not what we need. We don't need the new mobile phone. We just desire to replace it with the older version.

When Zarathustra informs us about our choices and increases our wisdom to choose, he is warning us about our wants and desires. He is not against human needs and desires; he is guiding us toward healthier and more beneficial ones.[8] Zarathustra never preached self-imposed suffering on us on our spiritual path. He believed that we are here on Earth to grow and be wise (vertical, spiritual) and to have a happy and joyful life (horizontal). The purpose of our lives is to make Earth like a paradise. We are not here to suffer, but to be happy. We are not created sinful, but out of goodness and love. Therefore, we need to live a good and joyful life on Earth.

Zarathustra believed that true happiness (peacefulness) occurs when we are in harmony (Asha) within and without. He was not against pleasure, but he warned us against choices made based on desires that will bring us pain and misery. Certain desires could lead us to a happy life, such as buying comfortable shoes for walking. Or they may make our lives miserable, such as addiction. One becomes obsessed with the constant desire arising from the addiction.

Devotion: Although we must meet our basic needs, and we want to fulfill certain desires—emotionally and intellectually—we require devotion and love to pursue the higher self and connect with our essence. This is the path of Mazdaism (*Mazda-Yasna*) and the teaching of Zarathustra. Mazdaism means being the devotee and the lover of wisdom. It is an inner work for those individuals who are willing to face themselves and find the seed of wisdom and consciousness within

---

8 Yasna 31.11

themselves, which was taught by Zarathustra himself and then later by the Magi (wise men and women) who followed his teaching. It is the path of those who are the flowers of wisdom.

We cannot pursue our higher self if we are entangled in our basic needs and earthly desires. Zarathustra calls this force the spirit of *Armaiti*. It is a higher spirit and force within that requires us to be awakened in order to motivate us toward our higher purpose and potential on Earth. *Armaiti* is the Spirit of Holy Serenity, Tranquility, Devotion, Holy Compliance, and Love, according to Zarathustra. It is a force above our needs, wants, and desires. It is the Holy Desire. It is devotion to knowing our true being and connecting with the Spirit of Spirits, the Sublime Spirit, Ahura Mazda.[9]

Zarathustra did not encourage people to suppress, destroy, or deny their desires. In fact, desires give spice and colour to our lives. Without desires, life would be very boring and dreadful. It is like eating food without any spices. It is not delicious, regardless of how healthy the food is. Is it nice to crave an ice cream while lying on the beach and enjoying the sunshine? Is it wonderful to desire having your beloved next to you and enjoying each other's company? Is it great to desire a career that you really enjoy or your own family and children? Then why do we need to remove ourselves from others, isolating ourselves in a cave or lying down on a bed of nails, suffering? Is there not enough suffering in the world? Zarathustra was against asceticism, or any self-imposed suffering.

You are not sinful because you have desires and are enjoying your life. Don't feel guilty because you have fully embraced

9   Yasna 33.13

your existence. Question yourself if you do not feel so. You are not born to suffer. You are born to be joyful and transform yourself to a higher human being. Have desires and enjoy life, but don't forget your higher purpose, the higher desire—devotion—to "know thyself." Knowing thyself, one begins to know Ahura Mazda, the Supreme Being. Have needs and desires, but don't get too entangled or distracted by your needs and desires. Focus on, and invest in, your self-realization as well.

Zarathustra doesn't want you to destroy or suppress your desires; he wants you to be purified and transform them to higher desires, such as seeking wisdom and love. Desires are like flowers in the garden of beings; but some desires are like weeds and dandelions, sucking and consuming all the forces of your being. He calls those desires that are destructive to your existence *Ahriman* (Satan in English). He calls the desire that brings a thirst and hunger to find your true being *Armaiti*—the spirit of love and devotion.

Armaiti, or the spirit of devotion, is like fuel to a spaceship. It helps it take off from the earth and surpass its force of gravity in order to get to space. Without that energy, the spaceship can never leave the earth. Through the force of devotion (*Armaiti*), we enter the space of pure consciousness. It is in that space that we can experience our true being. It gives us a different perspective, an opportunity to see ourselves from a wider view in our existence. It is like an astronaut looking at the earth from space. Similarly, with the higher self (essence), when we take off from the gravity of needs and desires, we see ourselves and our earthly personality from a wider perspective.[10]

---

10 Yasna 43.6

It is like someone sees the street from the first floor while someone else sees the same street from the fourth floor. Each looks at the same street at the same time, but each views it from a different perspective. The spirit of devotion and love (*Armaiti*) is the elevator or the stairs to take us to the fourth floor. We cannot just jump from other floors to the fourth one. We also require a higher desire to go to the fourth floor. If we are happy on the other floors, why bother? It takes effort and devotion to go there. Why do we need to go through all that effort? We feel secure, content, and familiar with the other floors and where we are. Why bother?

However, there may come a time when one develops a thirst, a hunger for it. The lower desires begin to feel like drinking water from the sea. It is salty. It does not quench one's thirst. The more one drinks from the lower desires, the more one becomes thirstier for spring water. It is like a blind person who sees a rainbow once his life. He becomes obsessed with the need to see it again. He devotes his entire life to seeing the light and the rainbow again. No other desire in his blindness will satisfy him again. This intense thirst for the higher self and wisdom is devotion.

The spirit of *Armaiti* is awakened in the person, according to Zarathustra. This thirst is often awakened by an event, a person, or idea. It can also be awakened internally by itself. It is like waking up in the morning naturally without any alarm clock. You just woke up. Just like that. It is like you are awake and you cannot go back to sleep again regardless of how much you tried. Eventually, you feel like you have insomnia. You cannot go back to sleep. You woke up to a thirst and desire within you that cannot be quenched until its desire is satisfied.

It is like falling in love. The lover seeks their beloved. No other needs or desires would satisfy the person except the fulfillment of their devotion. If the force of devotion to connect with a higher self is not awakened, there is no interest in growing higher. We are stuck in the lower level of self, to pursue our needs and wants. There is a saying that goes, "You can lead a horse to water, but you cannot force him to drink." There is no devotion in the person.[11]

Will: Needs, desires, and devotion are from within a person. But will is from above. We often mistakenly confuse will with determination, discipline, high motivation, ambition, and so on. But will is the desire of the Absolute, the Supreme Wisdom, the Spirit of Spirits. Will is like after the spaceship takes off from the gravity of the earth, it aligns with Earth's orbit. It does not need its own fuel anymore. Will is the Supreme's orbit. We do not have desires anymore. We now live our existence according to the will of the Supreme Wisdom. Will means surrendering your being to the Higher Being. There is no ego or personality left any longer. We are emptied from the self to the higher self.

In the will level, we don't have any more desires or devotion. We have will. To have will means surrounding the Will of the Absolute. Let it be the Absolute's will, not mine. One way to know the Absolute is to surrender to the Supreme Will. It is like dropping your luggage onto an escalator at the airport. You do not have to carry the luggage; it is carried by the escalator. It is not

---

11   Yasna 43.10

your effort; it is the Supreme Effort, like the orbit of the earth. Will means to let go of our own efforts. Let it be Mazda's will.

It is like when you book a plane ticket. You pack and go to the airport. You board the airplane and sit in your assigned seat. Then, all your efforts to bring yourself there are done. Now you are at the mercy of the pilot. There is nothing else you can do. All the passengers have surrendered themselves to the will and the power of the pilot to take them to their destination. The passengers are now passive. They are in the hands of the pilot. When we surrender ourselves to the highest level of our being, we are not the doer anymore. We are in the hands of the Supreme Being. This is called willpower. It is not our will, needs, or desires. We are in the orbit of the Supreme Wisdom.

The Attributes

Everything in existence has certain attributes. We can recognize or know something based on its attributes. The attribute of salt is salty and sugar is sweetness. We know that to bake a cake, we don't add salt to sweeten it. We add sugar because of its attributes. If we want to cool down our room, we don't buy a dishwasher for it. We buy an air conditioner. They each function based on their attributes. Similarly, if we want to know someone, we try to get to know their character and attributes.

Everything in the universe has attributes. For instance, the attribute of water is wet and liquid. The attribute of fire is light and warmth. The attribute of a rock is stillness and hardness. One way to know about fire is to know and experience its heat and light. To know water is to drink it or jump into its wetness and fluidity. In order for someone to know about love, one must fall in love. One cannot know about love by reading love stories or watching a romantic movie.

We are attracted to people whose character we like. And we are repulsed by those whom we don't like. We try to idolize people and admire their character, like movie stars. At times, we want to be like them. To know someone, we try to get close to them physically to examine them better. Or we try to learn about them by knowing their attributes and seeing whether we want to be with them or not. Zarathustra also points out seven attributes of Ahura Mazda for us to know.

The esoteric aspect of Zarathustra (Mazdaism) teaches the devotee to cleanse the self and work on bringing Ahura Mazda's attributes within the self. By developing fully those attributes, one can experience the presence of the Absolute. He calls the seven attributes of Ahura Mazda the *Amesha Spenta*, meaning Immortal holy or bounteous. We can find our essence and our true being when we experience these seven attributes within ourselves. Then, the experience of essence based on those qualities is not different from the Supreme Essence. In order to see the sun, one must expose oneself to the sun's illumination. Those seven attributes are the Supreme Wisdom's illumination to the universe and our existence, similar to the seven colours of a rainbow. The sunbeam is the same, but the manifestation of it is expressed differently.

Although awakening to this higher thirst and devotion is important on the journey of self-inquiry, one also requires a guide, teachings, or a description on how to pursue it. Zarathustra described to us an idea of what we must work on. He said that the Supreme Being (Ahura Mazda) has seven attributes to know about. Those seven attributes are:

1. Consciousness and Wisdom (Ahura Mazda's essence)
2. Progressive Mentality (Good Thought, Progressive Mind—*Vohuman* or *Bahman*)
3. Harmony (Balance, Law, Principal, Asha, Artha—art in English)
4. Willpower (*Shahrewar*—inner discipline and control)
5. Peace (devotion, love —*Armaiti*)
6. Perfection (*Khordad*—wholeness, integrity, health, and completion)
7. Eternal (*Murdad*—deathless, immortal)

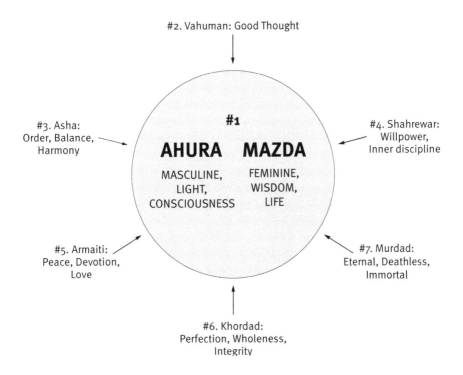

Figure #3. The *Amesha Spenta* (Immortal Bounteous):
Seven attributes of Ahura Mazda

There is gender equality in Zarathustra's approach. Men and women, masculine and feminine are addressed equally throughout his teaching.[12] Ahura is masculine, and Mazda is feminine. Of the six attributes of Ahura Mazda, three are masculine (*Vohuman*—good mind, *Asha*—balance and harmony, and *Shahrewar*—willpower) and three are feminine (*Armaiti*—peace and devotion, *Khrodad*—wholeness and perfection, and *Murdad*—immortality).

---

12 Yasna 30.2, Yasna 46.10

CHAPTER 3

The Seven Attributes of Ahura Mazda: The *Amesha Spenta*

1. Consciousness and Wisdom (Ahura Mazda)

Although the attributes of water are wetness and liquidity, H2O is the essence of it. Similarly, Ahura Mazda has several attributes, and consciousness and wisdom are its essence. Consciousness means awareness and being present. When one is conscious, one is fully aware and present. Usually, our sense of consciousness is accidental and momentous. When we observe ourselves, we realize that we are not present. We are caught in our thoughts, emotions, or bodily sensations. We are often in a state of disassociation with what is happening around us. We are present when we are doing something new, such as learning how to drive a car. The moment we have mastered it, we go on autopilot. We start driving without being aware of it. Similarly, we eat without being aware of eating, we walk, we talk, we brush our teeth. Observe yourself when you brush your teeth. You realize that you are brushing, but your mind is thinking about something else. You are not present.

The other occasion on which we become conscious is when something happens accidentally, and it brings us to the present time. You are eating your food in a restaurant, then the server drops the dishes on the floor. Everyone becomes conscious of the incident. Our memories are often associated with when we were present at some point of our lives. That is why painful memories are easier to remember than joyful ones. In pain, we are awake. How can you think about something else when you have a headache or a toothache? Or we learn to dissociate ourselves from painful memories, such as trauma. Since traumatic events are very painful and we cannot escape from them, we learn to be absent and dissociate ourselves from them, such as with post-traumatic stress disorder (PTSD). Then, we become absent and disconnected with what is happening around us even though the trauma is not happening any longer.

When Zarathustra says that the essence of Ahura Mazda is consciousness, it means it is fully and totally present. There is no absenteeism. There is no autopilot or dissociation. The Supreme Consciousness Being is consciousness itself. Ahura means consciousness. It is associated with masculine energy and light. When there is light, we can see. Light brings everything to our awareness. Light and consciousness bring everything to life and existence.

The other essence of the Supreme Being is Mazda. It means wisdom. It is associated with the feminine energy and spirit. It is symbolized as water. Ahura Mazda is the Source (essence) of all beings and wisdom. When we look at our universe and existence, we see that everything is based on wisdom. We don't need to go far to search for such wisdom. We can look at how our body functions, how we digest food, or circulate the blood. The earth moves around the sun so precisely, not randomly.

In contrast to thinking of God as a male, Ahura Mazda is neither masculine nor feminine. It is both and neither. They are interdependent Masculine energy needs to work on his consciousness, grounding, stability, and be a container. Feminine energy needs to work on her nourishing, wisdom, and aliveness. Both forces exist in each human being. This concept was developed further after Zarathustra in Tantra (*Shiva* and *Shakti*) and in Taoism (*Yin* and *Yang*). Wisdom (Mazda) needs consciousness to be seen and consciousness (Ahura) needs wisdom to shine upon it. Consciousness needs something to be conscious of. Ahura is conscious of its wisdom (Mazda). Ahura is the seer, and Mazda is the seen. Ahura Mazda is both the seer and the seen. it is the absolute consciousness and wisdom. As the presence of the light banishes darkness without any conflict, wisdom also overcomes ignorance by its presence. Light and wisdom always win over darkness and ignorance.

2. Progressive Mentality (*Vohuman or Bahman*—Good Thought):

Life is like a river. It is continuously moving, growing, and evolving. When we look at our lives and the past, it is like a dream. Existence is like a well. The water keeps coming from the source continuously. Have you ever felt like life has stopped? We may get stagnated and entangled with our thoughts, emotions, or past, but our life never stops. It keeps flowing. There is no such thing as past or future. We always live in the moment, the here and now. When we pay attention, we can never live in the past or in the future. Being in the here and now does not mean that we are frozen. Rather, our consciousness is observing and witnessing the ever-flowing life. We are born, and we will die one day. But life is never born, and it never dies. It keeps flowing, growing, and evolving.

One of the most important attributes of Ahura Mazda's is *Vohuman* (progressive mentality and thought). Every creation from an artist begins with a thought. That is why Good Thought is the first ethical principle of Zarathustra, before the word and deed. Thoughts are the foundation of our words and actions. Therefore, we need to always be aware of the quality and the nature of our thoughts. Are our thoughts progressive, conscious, and based on wisdom, or are they wicked, stagnated, and destructive?

Zarathustra speaks of a twin force in the human mind. The first one is *Spenta Mainyu,* the good mind (sacred wisdom, Holy Spirit in Christianity) which wants to pull us to a higher consciousness (wisdom). This is the force of progression. The other force is called *Angra Mainyu,* the wicked mind (*Ahriman,* evil). This internal force wants to pull us down to ignorance and to an unconscious life. The concept Mainyu simply means mind, spirit, or thought.[13]

Spenta is the energy and the mind of creativity, growth, wisdom, and goodness. Spenta means "to expand, swell, increase, progress." *Angra* (anger in English) is the mind and energy of destruction, stagnation, chaos, or disorder. According

---

13 Yasna 30.3

to Zarathustra, everything in existence is in pairs. He calls them twin spirits. These two forces are not opposite to each other or in a cosmic struggle, they are neutral and exist in the human mind. The work of every human is to channel their thoughts toward a good and progressive mind and stay away from the wicked mind.

Good Thought (*Vohuman*) is the progressive mentality and the force behind the change toward growth and evolvement. This change is eternal and permanent. Except for the change, everything else in the universe keeps changing and evolving. There is no such thing as to "be." Everything is in the process of "becoming." To be means to just exist and be static. *Vohuman*'s force in life moves the world into becoming more and more. Even a table or a rock is not static. There is a movement and an invisible dynamic that is happening between their molecules. Nothing is at rest. Everything is in a process of flow and change toward its growth and its full potential.

The mind is powerful. Our thoughts determine our state of being. There are many thoughts from which we can choose. There are good thoughts, wise thoughts, loving thoughts, and compassionate thoughts. There are also wicked thoughts, foolish thoughts, and vicious thoughts. What kinds of thoughts we choose to have in our minds will impact our words and behaviours. They determine who we become.

As humans, we also need to attune ourselves to a progressive life and a conscious mind. We go astray and live in deception if our mind is disconnected from the Supreme's mind.[14]

14 Yasna 31.6

3. Harmony (*Asha*—Balance, Law, Order, Arta: Art in English)

The third attribute of Ahura Mazda is Asha (art) meaning order, the divine intelligence and reason in existence. *Asha* is a complex and orderly force and intelligence ruling the universe. When one looks deeply into existence, there is no chaos. The universe functions based on certain principles, order, harmony, and rhythm. *Asha* represents the universal divine principles regulating both the physical and the spiritual worlds. Science means to discover and use this pre-existing force for our own purposes. For example, Newton did not create the law of gravity. However, by discovering this law, we can now fly an airplane. We can send a satellite to orbit Earth. If the universe were based on chaos or disorder, we would not have any scientific discovery.

If this pre-existing law and order kept changing every day and there was not any regulation, we would not have night and day, the change of seasons, or knowing at what temperature water freezes or boils. Because of this precise law and wisdom in existence, there is a certain predictability in it. We know that water does not boil one day at 60° Celsius and another day at 95° Celsius. One does not need to go too far to understand this. We can look at our own physical functioning and the wisdom behind our blood circulation, digestion, immune system, or the brain's complexity to realize *Asha*.

Science means that the universe functions in a consistent and predictable way. It functions rationally and intelligently. Chaos is a human creation and interferes with the existence of orderly fashion. If we look deeply into life, we find laws and order (*Asha*). Discovering those laws gives us insight into the mysteries of the universe and a Higher Being (Ahura Mazda).[15]

While *Vohuman* is associated with the Divine's Good Thought, *Asha* is represented as the Right Deeds and Action. Righteousness means to channel our actions and behaviours similar to Ahura Mazda (the Divine Intelligence). An individual who follows the path of *Asha* will eventually attain eternal light and immortality. *Asha* is the law of existence. In order to have a healthier life, we need to be tuned in and live under the same laws and principles. Deviation from these laws will bring chaos and disharmony into our lives.

4. Willpower (*Shahrewar*—Inner Discipline and Control)

Willpower was discussed in the previous chapter. First, we need to distinguish willpower from will to power. Will to power is egocentric, selfish, and it is based on dominating others. Since we don't know who we really are, and associate ourselves with our personality, we want to be someone or something special and be different from others. We want to be somebody important who is better, higher, and holier than others. Will to power is our struggle to control others since we may feel special, privileged, and unique. There is a desire within that people look up to us. This is a human's deep inferiority complex. We seek to feel powerful, to get recognition, status, acknowledgment, respect, and control. We may seek to be powerful because it boosts our ego. Power nourishes our false identity like food. A

---

15 Yasna 31.13

powerful person can destroy others who challenge or question their ego or self-importance. The Divine Being does not have this need.

Willpower means one's true being is in charge. There is an inner clarity. There is no doubt or hesitation. One knows exactly what one wants and acts upon it. Willpower comes from knowing and seeing. One walks and sees a wall. They open the door to go outside rather than hitting the wall or jumping out the window. The decision is very clear because they can see and decide accordingly. Willpower is not like disciplining ourselves to quit smoking or go to the gym. That is called self-discipline. Willpower is when one knows smoking is not healthy and has the clarity to not be tempted to pollute their lungs. As mentioned previously, since we are not conscious human beings, we don't have much willpower. Most of our actions are based on desires, attractions, and repulses.

Since Ahura Mazda is the Supreme Consciousness, there is no doubt, temptation, or hesitation. All thoughts, words, and actions come from the Absolute Knowing. Ahura Mazda thinks, talks, and acts precisely and according to its willpower. The holy reasoning and wisdom create *will* in us that is expressed through our words and actions. The practice of good thoughts, good words, and good deeds creates a higher value and willpower in our existence. Ahura Mazda also gave willpower to humans to not live robotically or animalistically, but rather to choose and determine our lives based on wisdom. We are given the ability to distinguish between right and wrong and channel our will toward goodness rather than wickedness. This gift of choice requires us to increase our consciousness.

Willpower without goodness and wisdom can lead us toward will to power, domination, and wickedness.[16]

5. Peace (*Armaiti*—Love, Devotion)

As discussed in the previous chapter, *Armaiti* means virtue, devotion, piety, tranquility, and serenity. *Spenta Armaiti* is a feminine entity. It is the virtues of service and loving-kindness. The spirit of *Armaiti* guides and protects the devotees on their spiritual path. It symbolizes inner peace and love toward others. She is known and plays a role as "Mother Nature" in our existence.

Peace only occurs when there is inner tranquility. It happens when there is no fracture, duality, tension, or hesitation. We can only feel peaceful when there is inner harmony and integrity. It is like being at a concert and hearing all the musicians play their instruments harmoniously. Illness is when there is a disturbance in an organ's functioning, or the body is not in harmony within or externally. Disease can occur when the kidney does not filter the toxins properly, or when the skin is exposed to too much sunlight. Peace does not mean resting, being comfortable, or having a nice meal. Peace means being balanced, unified, and holistic. Peace comes after good thoughts, wisdom, consciousness, willpower, balance, and order. We cannot be peaceful when we live in chaos, hesitation, having wicked thoughts, or when our surroundings are disturbed.

---

16 Yasna 30.2

We feel peace when there is no agitation, restlessness, unmet desires, uncertainty, confusion, or illness. There is a sense of tranquility, equilibrium, and contentment. We are calmed, settled, and rested. Peacefulness is another attribute of Ahura Mazda since the mind is pure (*Vohuman*). There is absolute consciousness and wisdom. There is balance and harmony within and without (*Asha*). There is no hesitation or doubt. Ahura Mazda has willpower. The attribute of peacefulness exists because of these foundations. Without them, one can never be peaceful. The state of peacefulness is also called paradise, or heaven.[17]

6. Perfection (*Khordad*—Wholeness, Integrity, Health, and Completion)

When we use the word "I," it means there are many "I's" within. We think that we have a singular integrated sense of self. That is wrong. When we look at ourselves, we are many. There is a crowd inside each of us. One minute, we decide on something. Another minute, we change our mind. We feel something now and feel differently in a short time. We play a role based on our circumstances in one situation, such as being a husband. We may have a totally different personality in a different context, such as being at work. However, in Ahura Mazda, there is no fracture. There is no sub-personality. Ahura Mazda is one, whole, integrated, complete, and perfect. It is perfect and absolute consciousness and wisdom. There is no division. It is an absolute state of unity and wholeness. Ahura Mazda does

17 Yasna 47.3

not need to complete and perfect itself. It is already perfect in all dimensions.

7. Eternal (*Murdad*—Deathless, Immortal)

We don't have any concept of boundlessness and eternity. Life on Earth is based on time and space. We measure most things according to these two frameworks. We measure time in a very linear way, from the past to the future or from the future to now. However, there is another state beyond time. It is eternity. It is timeless.

Most of our sense of time comes from Earth's rotation on its axis and around the sun. Imagine that Earth always remains the same distance from the sun and never moves. Half of it is facing the sun permanently, and the other half is away from the sun in the darkness. In this position, how could we have a sense of time? What does night and day mean, or summer and winter? How could we measure the time if we always face the sun? If we don't have watches or clocks, is there time without the movement of Earth? We would have a sense of timelessness.

The moment we become conscious of our true self, we are no longer mortals. The body dies, but a part of us similar to Ahura Mazda is deathless and immortal. There is a beginning to a wave in the ocean and there is an end to it. But does the wave really die, or does it become the ocean again? Eternal means that there is no beginning and there is no end. It is the alpha and the omega. The best description of eternity is the concept of a circle. Where can we say the beginning or the end of a circle is? Eternity is related to timelessness, while infinity is associated with a number. One way to grasp the idea of eternity is through infinity in numbers. We can go from -1, -2, -3, -4, to +1, +2, +3, +4. It is endless.

In the symbol of fravashi which is the eternal spirit within us, the central circle around its trunk symbolizes that our spirit, similar to Ahura Mazda, is immortal, having neither a beginning nor an end.

Conclusion

Remember the story of Tarzan, who grew up among apes? The plane that was carrying him as a child with his family crashed in the jungle, and his family died. He survived, and the apes raised him. He began to believe that he was an ape. That is all he knew. When other humans found him in the jungle, he could not comprehend that he was a human and not an ape. It was difficult for Tarzan to accept that. His previous identity collapsed. He needed to let go of his false self in order to reconstruct it again from a different point of view. Likewise, each of us—if we wish to grow—need to face up to the stories and tales that we have borrowed for a time to represent who we are in our lives.

Are we who we really are, like Tarzan, and have we forgotten our true identity (a conscious human being)? A new reality of our identity must emerge to set us free from our illusion. Tarzan woke up to his true reality. He was a human being. Likewise, we all need to realize that we all have a higher purpose for our existence. There is a higher being within each of us who needs to be awakened, cultivated, and evolved.

Buddha means "the awakened one." His real name was Siddhartha. After many years of effort, he woke up from his delusion and found his higher being—Buddhahood. Siddhartha was a prince living a comfortable and luxurious life until one day he realized that all the comforts that he had were impermanent. He walked away from his false security and purpose in life and went after his true being, that which "never dies, never is sick, and never ages." He found the eternal and permanent part of his being at last. He said afterward that if he can be a Buddha, we all can wake up and become a Buddha (the awakened one) as well.

Zarathustra taught this same truth centuries before him: *"Be the light and shine light to others like a candle flame."* Zarathustra taught us that in order to know the light, we must be the light. Shine your light to others as well. Since you are light, it is not different from the Supreme Light. It is like the moon reflecting sunlight to Earth in the darkness of the night.

Our light and consciousness are fragmented. There is a very limited part of us that is conscious. A greater part in us remains unconscious. The light (Ahura) within us is hidden while we live in the darkness of our ignorance, deception, illusion, and unconsciousness. We are not one piece. We live in duplicity— the true self vs. the false (personality). As long as the consciousness in us is not awakened, we live fragmented—in division, chaos, and disorder. We can be whole and integrated when we are united within and become one. Otherwise, our existence is like an iceberg. We only have access to a small portion of our potential. Most of our being is hidden underneath, deep in darkness.

We humans are born good, but incomplete. Our purpose on Earth is to improve ourselves by moving from ignorance to consciousness, from chaos to order and harmony, from desires and repulsion to willpower, from multiplicity of selves to integration as one true being (*fravashi*—authentic self, essence), from mortality to immortality, from hate or anger to love and devotion, and from imperfection to perfection. Consciousness means to be totally aware and present. Our state of consciousness is very limited and scattered. When we observe ourselves, we realize that we are not awake, but on autopilot going through life robotically and mechanically based on familiarity, patterns, desires, and comfort.

There is a degree of consciousness that we experience. We need to focus on the duration and frequency of consciousness in our daily existence. First, we need to try to increase the frequency of our consciousness. We are required to catch ourselves frequently when we are absent and unconscious. This exercise is called self-remembering. We can self-remember ourselves while eating, walking, watching TV, listening to others, etc. It is like driving at night and keeping watch so as not to fall asleep.

Second, we need to practise the duration of our consciousness. It may happen only for a few seconds at a time. However, we can put effort into staying present and awake longer each time. We can increase the duration of the consciousness. Third, we need to increase the intensity and the degree of our consciousness as we are practising. The intensity of the consciousness can be increased by fully observing what is happening outside of us. At the same time, we are watching our body language, thoughts, inner words, and emotions. For instance, when we are listening to someone's story, we can watch ourselves internally as well as how the other person's communication is impacting us internally.

This inner separation between the observer (the true self, consciousness, awareness) and the observed (the subject of observation) needs to happen in order to grow and develop consciousness. Meditation does not mean to sit somewhere quietly, with crossed legs, straight back, watching our breath or candlelight. Meditation means being aware and present with what we do or don't do at a particular moment of our lives. Meditation is not an activity. Rather, it is letting go and disidentifying the self from the activities in order to remain a witness. To meditate means to be present and to be an observer.

Our path toward growth and perfection is to move away from personality in order to develop and awaken the essence. In fact, we don't have a personality. Each person has many personalities depending on their role, circumstance, age, environment, emotional state, or crisis. In meditation or observation, one returns to their origin, the essence, the authentic self. It is the state where the mind does not wander in a thousand directions and jumps from one thought to another like monkeys moving from one tree to another. Consciousness is in charge, and the attention does not get lost in things. Rather, it stays centred at home within itself like a mirror. Subjects come to it.

Although Western psychotherapy and mental health practitioners can help us with our immediate crises, daily struggles, or mental, emotional, behavioural, or relational dysfunctions, they can't take us deeper into our existence. The aim of Western psychotherapy is to make someone functional in society or in their personal life. However, it doesn't take us past further empowering our personality. In fact, the focus of psychotherapy is to strengthen someone's ego (identity) in order to function better within their struggles. In order to know ourselves beyond our earthly identity with the higher self (essence), it is essential to study Eastern perspective and learn from the teachings of wisdom keepers in history, such as Zarathustra, Yeshua (Jesus), Buddha, Lao Tzu, and many others.

Similar to the people who were trying to bring Tarzan to his own true nature, these teachers taught us to remember the Divine Light and the consciousness within each of us. They challenged us not to be content with who we are, but to strive for who we can become. Their teachings are not based on being and just existing. They taught us the path of becoming and looking at our potential. They encouraged us to transform ourselves from a caterpillar to a butterfly and from water to wine. They were not just teachers to inform us of basic knowledge. They were alchemists who came to transform us to higher substances.

Humans differ from animals since we are given the gift of choice to determine our destiny. We are free to choose ignorance or wisdom, right or wrong, good or bad, to vegetate or to grow, to be fractured or whole. The choice is ours, but we also need willpower, thirst, interest, devotion, wisdom, principles, and integrity.

There is a difference between knowing something and knowing about something. Knowing something is one's direct experience and wisdom. Knowing about something is getting information about something without experiencing it. For instance, one can learn about aviation and how to fly an airplane from a book without ever sitting in an airplane or flying it. Zarathustra is not content to teach us about the Absolute. He wants us to experience Ahura Mazda within our own consciousness. He suggests one way to know the Divine Being is through its seven attributes: consciousness and wisdom, good thought, balance and order, willpower, devotion and peacefulness, perfection, and deathlessness.

To know oneself from Zarathustra's point of view is not about our job, talent, appearance, social class, intelligence, gender, wealth, or status. To know oneself means to know Ahura Mazda within us. To know oneself means to know the seed of consciousness that needs to be cultivated in order to grow and produce the fruits of a true human being. In order to do so, one is required to eliminate who they are by identifying with their personality and connecting with their essence. It is a path of cleansing and purifying the self from who we are not in order to remember who we truly are.

We can experience the Supreme Being when we don't exist any longer. We become one with the Higher Being. The river has merged with the ocean. The person becomes empty of everything and all the self-identities. Once a Persian king offered a feast to everyone. He invited the poor and the richest people into his palace to attend. Everyone sat down according to their social status. The poor sat below near the door, the landowners sat above them, then the merchants, ministers, and the prime minister. The king was supposed to sit on his throne above all the guests.

A mystic walked to the palace while everyone was waiting for the king to come, and he did not sit with the poor, nor with the rich, nor the ministers. He kept walking up, passing every-one, when the guards stopped him. They asked him who he thought he was. Was he above the rich or the ministers? The mystic said that he was above them. Then, they asked him if he was above the prime minister and the king. He said that he was above them. They told him that only God is above the king. Was he God? He said that he was above God. They all laughed and told him there is nothing above God. The mystic said, "That is true, and that is me: I AM NOTHING."

This is true. When one is, God is absent. When one is gone, God is present. Then, there is no longer a person in the body. They become the light. The same light that shines in the universe.

The light shapes the very essence of all that exists. It is the fundamental energy and consciousness that underlies the fabric of reality. This light is not merely a physical illumination, but a metaphorical representation of awareness, understand-ing, and higher consciousness. It symbolizes the divine spark within every living being and signifies a deeper connection to the spiritual and universal aspects of existence.

MAY THE MAZDA SPIRIT OF LOVE
AND WISDOM ALWAYS BE OUR GUIDE

www.zarathustra.ca